Twenty Pandemicals

Twenty Pandemicals

Poems by

Charlotte Innes

Charlotte Innes

For Leslie,

with much love,

Charlotte

El Cholo
Santa Monica
May 6, 2022

Cover design by Shay Culligan
Cover Art "Framed 1" by Annie Clavel
Author photograph by Brian Gilmartin

ISBN: 978-1-63980-061-2

Kelsay Books
502 South 1040 East, A-119
American Fork, Utah 84003
Kelsaybooks.com

I dedicate this book to dear friends who gave me much-needed support throughout the pandemic with frequent phone calls, emails, online chats, happy hours and distanced walks.

I am especially grateful to Helen Benedict, Wendy Klein, Quincy Lehr, Pat Parkin-Moore and Joe Wakelee-Lynch.

And here's to the musicians who kept me sane, especially two American folk-rock bands, Caamp and Trampled by Turtles.

i.m. Lizzie (2001–2020).

Acknowledgments

I am grateful to the following journals for publishing the poems listed below:

Live Encounters: "Pandemical #6"
The Orchards Poetry Journal: "Pandemical #1" (as "Pandemical")

An Amaranthine Summer: A Collection of Poems and Stories
(Kelsay Books, 2021) dedicated to the memory of poet Kim
Bridgford who died on June 28, 2020: "Pandemical #14"

Special thanks are due to Rick Mullin who read through the manuscript of *Twenty Pandemicals* and gave me extensive comments on individual poems and on the book as a whole.

Gratitude to Amanda Koenigsberg, Nancy Murphy and Hilda Weiss for reading through an earlier version of the manuscript and offering excellent advice and support.

Much love and thanks to Sarah Maclay and the poets in The Nightbirds poetry workshop who prompted me to produce many of the "pandemicals," and whose encouragement and friendship helped me through the summer into the fall of 2020, and beyond.

Contents

Pandemical #1

At this time, I am resisting cleaning
closets filled with stuff I ought to junk,
old clothes, old shoes that have no worth or meaning,
unlike my neighbors who methodically plunk

their relics curbside, with notes on shelves
or gunky tables, saying "Free!" when it's
the owners who are trying to free themselves
from fear or boredom, I suspect, with a blitz

of order, ordering what they can, in this hell
of a world turned topsy-turvy by inert
invaders that come to life inside our cells,
that can't be cleaned away. For them, we're pay dirt.

Dirt. Relics. I can live with cat litter strewn
on rugs, old files and paper bugs call home.
What gets me is this sly virus goon
who stuffs my brain with blanks like packing foam.

Pandemical #2

The dumps. Not unconnected with this plague,
or the endless lies we hear from politicians.
Sorry if this sounds a little vague.
The thing is, where's the hope? No intermissions

halt the forward march of hate. And the wily
virus, every year or so, invents
a new stylish uniform and quietly
slips inside us. His new weapon dents

our poor old lungs, our hearts, our eyes, our feet
again. And again we hide away at home,
or don our masks to shop, which seems a treat
after online chats or having to comb

the Web for toilet paper. Will this be our lives,
forever and ever amen? With a devilish plot
at every turn, rotting our will to survive?
Ah, the dumps. There've always been ways to be got.

Pandemical #3

A coiled sleepy dragon winds around
the store, stirring now and then to inch
forward. Intrepid shoppers! Not one downed
by noonday heat. A woman tries to pinch

the spot in front of me. We smile. So what?
She's gaunt, limping. Besides, we have distraction,
phones, texting, emails. One guy who's got
a book is so engrossed, his satisfaction

seeps along the line. Though masked and spread
apart, tense from daring to venture out,
we become celebrants of *not dead yet,*
of deep blue sky, of rained-on grass about

as green as party garlands, until at last,
the entrance to the treasure house. A man,
oldish, flower in hair—he's having a blast—
doles out the wipes then, bright-eyed, lets us in.

Pandemical #4

How lovely, peach carnations! The first flowers
I've bought since March. Why now? The end of June
this year is not exactly cheering. Hours
at home. The brooding silence. Then delusion.

I mean that sense of joy when you decide
you must get out, go drink with friends. Or hold
a party. Some protest. It's time to fight
for the right to shop—or crush the hate. Resolve

to refute lies. Everyone wants "the truth."
A hoax! Or China's chemical war on us!
Or: Defund police! Re-teach our youth!
Heed science! Acknowledge racist violence!

To kill a living creature isn't right.
People or cows. OK, I love beef stew
but wince to see raw meat. Cut flowers die
a slow death. My peach carnations droop.

Pandemical #5

Doctors say the lungs of those near death
from Covid fill with holes *like Swiss cheese,*
so graphic a phrase, it almost stops my breath.
And it's not a cheese I like. This disease

is more of a young Fontina, I would say,
small-eyed, rich, nuttier. I'd rather think of
cake. I know. There's one with a perfect name,
Fanouropita, the Cake for Lost Things,

for the Greek Saint Phanourios to whom
you pray if you lose a thing that means a lot,
for whom you bake, if it's found, and for whom
you eat a cake that's a mix of oil and orange.

Fittingly, he was a man who knew sweetness,
in his love of God, but also bitter strife,
tortured to death for his beliefs. In these
cheesy times, who'd sacrifice a life?

Pandemical #6

Naked again, she twirls along my street,
sits down in traffic, picks up stones like plums,
inspects them, throws them away. Katha screams,
Miguel, Miguel, where are you, Miguel? He comes

at last, lays down a blanket and they sleep,
unless they're high. Then it's a night of curses,
screams. By morning, the sidewalk's inches deep
with litter. For Miguel and Katha, home. For us

sheltered people, already fearful enough,
their life's a deluge flooding ours, a madness
we can't control—for all our meetings. It's rough.
The screams break us apart, ignite old sadness.

Worried for our health, we envision viral
droplets filling the air. Two people, I tell
myself, of hundreds. All the numbers spiral.
To the East, more madness. This won't end well.

Pandemical #7

In the beginning, there was complete silence.
Even mockingbirds sang not a single note.
Cars, undriven. People, at home. An absence.
A time when Chaos ruled not too remote,

like Ragnarök when the Midgard serpent woke,
unwound its coils from round the earth, soaring
out of the ocean, spitting venom to choke
people and gods with unbreathable air, unmooring

the ocean to cover the land, till Thor killed it,
then died himself. For some, the story goes
that land appeared again or God willed it,
fresh, green, with people who, I suppose,

knew nothing of the ways a world might end.
Now, enraged by a virus you can't beat down,
or, impatient to live, killing a friend,
sense the serpent's shadow, prepare to drown.

Pandemical #8

My stepson notes his dad, that is, my ex,
died three years ago today. He's tagged
his mum, my ex's widow, and me. He says,
thinking of family today. I'm dragged

teary-eyed through all my deaths, his death,
my dad's, my cat's, the death of my best friend,
and what I thought I had discarded, shibboleths
creeping in like little deaths. No end

to *should-I-haves?* Or *shouldn'ts.* I know, of course,
no matter what I should or shouldn't have done,
it's done. I'm awed by my stepson's grace. Flaws
be damned. Now, in this time of death, let's shun

the dark, let's think of beautiful souls tonight,
cures for sadness, something slant, old scars
that signal mending, the cool folk-rock I like,
a rough-edged voice, a banjo bright as stars.

Pandemical #9

"After the cabbages had created plates,
and eaten themselves by candlelight for lunch,
the jailers cheered," Old Topsy said. "That spate
of rustling, numbers off—they'd had a hunch

that I, their Top Cabbage, was getting lax.
But I'm no fool. That's why we needed plates,
the ritual sacrifice, the important pact:
Some die and the little cabbages escape."

Old Topsy said the time had come, foretold
on ancient leaves, when cabbages would take
their rightful place as kings of all the globe.
"We'll multiply," he said, "make poisonous fakes

on which the people choke. And once the peeps
are dead, we cabbages will rule. In style!
On leafy thrones!" So I said, "No more need
for plates and fakes?" Old Topsy winked and smiled.

Pandemical #10

Let's boot the lizard up the chimney—like Alice
who grew too tall inside the rabbit's house.
Of course, she didn't do it out of malice.
She thought it through and knew she had to pounce

before it got to her. Sensible child,
also kind, polite, honest, worrying
about the over-sensitive mouse she'd riled
by praising her cat as a catcher, which sent him scurrying.

We need those boots and Alice's scorn of lies—
the Hatter, the Duchess, the Queen. If only we
could see the world as clearly, if only our guys,
so-called guardians of morality,

could see their own fake faces, we could yell,
like Alice, "You're nothing but a pack of cards!"
and laugh our joyous socks off as they fell,
unmasked, flattened, hoist with their own petards.

Pandemical #11

A starving deer is trying to nibble a tree
scorched black by fire. She cannot see what was
no longer is. Not a single juicy leaf,
only what can't be eaten. Flecks of ash,

filling the air, covering streams and stumps
and hills for miles. A grey plague smothering
wild places. It's like what's killing us
inside our bodies. The world is suffering,

the world is sick, and seen or unseen, changed.
Hotter, with seas lifting, animals dying.
Inside, time and place seem re-arranged.
But wasn't it always so? Once, driving

with my father past my dear old school,
I saw no trim front lawns but weeds waist-high.
In shock, my eye went up the slope. The school,
no longer there. An empty space. The sky.

Pandemical #12

There was a summer, wasn't there? No rain
to soften the heart or stop the fires. Our state
was almost burned to bits but now it's feigning
normalcy. I'm hearing birds of late,

chatter about the vote, the swamp, various
aspects of natural order. Same old, you know?
Like senators who say, nefariously,
they keep their scorn for *him* a secret. So.

Lies plus loathsome votes add up to little.
The ship is listing. When people think that heads
might roll—ha!—allegiance becomes quite brittle.
In fact, it's been a sorry summer, the deaths

go on and on. One head *really* rolled,
one governor almost shot. And R.B.G…
Here's where I stop, recalling only the bold,
some songs, a gleam of seaweed. Anything pretty.

Pandemical #13

Happiness has its place. We simply need
not to be silly about it. Don't say, *darkness,
no other way.* Sure, grey clouds. Always
a sign of doom in California, right?

But maybe they're more a call for gentleness,
especially now. *Ha!* They're like a massive
duvet, soft and full of feathers. *Or foam.*
Yes…a place to read or stroke the cat.

You mean, we'll all be dead soon enough?
Exactly. So. Enjoy…*You're so deluded!
We've had these clouds for days. Besides, they're yellow.*
Unusual, yes. From fires, perhaps? You know,

the sun will soon be back. Let's breathe. Oh wait,
that's tasteless. Sorry. Well. Just think of clouds
as compost out of which French marigolds
might bloom! Don't roll your eyes. OK. Let's talk.

Pandemical #14

The village I cannot visit now slides
in glimpses through my thoughts, the cows grazing
meadows by the River Soar that lie
across from a field where my father's aging

into earth, his quiet body giving
way at last to what we're all made of.
I'm oddly shaken to think my body's a living
piece of him, so he's still here, laid

to rest, but living on in me. Cliché
you'd think, but having felt so separate for
so long (*My life! My life!*) I cannot say
what all this means to me, except that more

of me is *there* than I had thought. But oh,
I want to see the village, my stepmother's garden,
to hear the blackbird's song, to smell a rose,
clink *cheers* and talk of jaunts we might embark on.

Pandemical #15

Another fire and the sky's gone yellow again.
There is no other way way to say this but
another fire and the sky's gone yellow again.
It's hard to resist a striking symbol but

skip the apocalyptic stuff for these
truths, kids in cages, teargas, lying.
It's no surprise that many have tried to seize
the day, with books and speeches, but we're dying

and every word's a splash of blood with no-one
stanching wounds on the daily canvas. Brown
and black predominate so seeing the bones
of it almost can't be done. There's a clown,

I think, a circus scene, some magic tricks
to distract the dying crowd, and a flying trapeze
bearing a child wielding shadows. Transfixed,
the crowd screams *lock!* And conjures hate disease.

Pandemical #16

Here's a way to look at lack of trust:
burn your mask, as some Floridians did,
in a ceremony, like those who once burned books
they thought degenerate. The untrusting heart

can only melt so much. After burning up
with love, and losing it, the untrusting heart
turns cold, though it burns with anger. Daddy's pawn
burns early and withers in its little pot.

Daddy's pawn needs adoration day
and night and tells the adoring audience
that he adores them. He says what he thinks
they want to hear. He jokes because he knows

that laughter feels like love. And once they've laughed,
they'll die for him. I've burned for love. I know
that demon need. I've lost my trust. I burn
for those deceived by ice who'd burn us all.

Pandemical #17

We're all sunk in the Slough of Despond, the Lake
of Tears, these dullard months of staying home,
watching the death-toll rise, missing friends.
Mr. Grifter was voted out but still

he's spreading lies, toxic as the toxins
wasting poor old Lizzie as her kidneys
fail. My cat, nineteen. She barely eats.
Just wait, I whisper, till a good man comes.

The lies. The tears. The lies. I cannot take
the steady drool of news from papers, phone,
my inbox. Corruption fills the air like ash,
like carrion birds awaiting someone's death.

But oh, with Grifter voted out, the tears
of relief, of joy, the honking cars, dancing
in the streets. One day. And we the people
glowed. As if the Messiah had come at last.

Pandemical #18

But he, the man who dances on a dime,
who says one thing and then its opposite
immediately, who wriggles out of every
sticky situation, who's sticky, sticking

to our days. Please leave, we beg. We want
to swing on porches, even if we haven't
got a porch, to rock and watch the clouds,
black and white, patch up this haunted blue,

to ignore all the angry faces, those
who always want someone to hate or blame,
for ragged nails, untended hair, gym
closures, who want to think that Mistah Weak

can save them all, even though his hurting
heart can only hurt them more. There'll be
no savior soon. Or ever. The world's burning
like—I'll say it—the fires of Armageddon.

Pandemical #19

My neighbor's olive trees have grown six feet
above the six-foot fence, breeze-blown branches
leaning languidly towards the street,
their tops sturdy and still above the glancing

flutter. Soon, like full-grown boys, they'll thicken,
heavier limbs, leaves more dense, long
fingers of silver-green. They rarely sicken.
Some live, bear fruit, 2,000 years, so strong

that people call them "tree of life." Who'd not
take comfort from so resolute a being?
The fence keeps thieves at bay, the house, all but
hidden, safe behind its wall of green.

Safe? From every threat? A tangled notion
like the olive of which God said, this tree
of "goodly fruit" must burn. The people had broken
their word, worshipped idols. Just wait. You'll see.

Pandemical #20

Yesterday, first time in months, I walked
the empty beach, undone by the air's freshness,
salt on my lips, the little sea-washed shells
almost bleached of color, by the wash-wash

of the waves, the tide providing tiny morsels
for waiting birds, by a flock of seagulls suddenly
rising, whirling and dipping till one of them snatched
a fish, or something, and clamorous shrieks arose

from squads of hungry bombers hurtling towards it,
by a row of sandpipers matching themselves
to the scalloped edge of a wave, eyeing the pullback,
running and pecking the drenched sand in search

of what's invisible to us, waiting
again, holding the place they've always held,
scholars gathering daily to parse the ocean's
endless argument on weight and froth.

Notes

"Framed 1," the original art on the cover of *Twenty Pandemicals,* is one of a sequence called "100 Petite Works and Boxes Installation" by Annie Clavel who challenged herself to complete a hundred tiny artworks (7"x5" paintings and tiny boxes) when the pandemic began in 2020. She painted every day for four months. "Framed 1" was created in January 2020.

A distinguished artist, originally from Paris, France, Clavel now lives and works in Long Beach, California. In a description of her work, she says: "Annie Clavel is not only an artist but also a trained mathematician. Her work derives from mathematical concepts, such as fractals, organized in terms of colors, shapes, light, and movement. Underlying her work are patterns: patterns of thoughts, emotions, and stories. The order underlying the chaos."

I chose "Framed 1" for my cover because it seems to reflect a similar framing of chaos in my pandemicals.

You can find out more about Annie Clavel and her work on her website: annieclavel.com

"Pandemical #5:" The comparison of lungs damaged by Covid-19 with "Swiss cheese" was noted on medical sites and in various journals and newspapers in 2020. The reference I saw was in a Washington Post story about a young woman who had a lung transplant (June 11, 2020).

"Pandemical #5:" *Fanouropita,* the Cake for Lost Things, and the Greek Saint Phanourios are a part of the Greek Orthodox religious tradition. I am indebted to Alicia Stallings for the recipe of this cake, which I have made. It is delicious.

"Pandemical #9" and "Pandemical #10:" these poems were inspired by the work of Lewis Carroll, that is, the novel *Alice's Adventures in Wonderland* and the poem "The Walrus and the Carpenter," which appears in the novel *Through the Looking Glass*.

"Pandemical #12:" the lines "One head *really* rolled, / one governor almost shot" refer to a French middle school teacher, Samuel Paty, who was beheaded by a radical Islamist after he had shown the *Charlie Hebdo* 2012 cartoons of Muhammad in a class about freedom of speech. The governor who was "almost shot" is Michigan's Democratic governor Gretchen Whitmer who narrowly missed being kidnapped and possibly killed by a group of extremist militia men. The plot was discovered, and the men arrested and indicted—and in one case sentenced. Further federal and state trials are currently pending.

"Pandemical #12:" "R.B.G." refers to Ruth Bader Ginsberg who served on the Supreme Court of the United States from 1993 to her death in September 2020. Late in life, she became an icon of popular culture and was often referred to as R.B.G. or "The Notorious R.B.G." after the rapper "The Notorious B.I.G."

"Pandemical #19:" the final stanza refers to a story in The Bible about the prophet Jeremiah (Jeremiah 11:1-17 KJV).

Afterword

...hot ice and wondrous strange snow!

Like many poets writing during the pandemic, after a period of malaise, I wrote my twenty pandemicals in a big rush, in just over six months, from May 1 to November 19, 2020. It helped that I was in an online poetry workshop over the summer with good poets I know well. But it seemed odd to me that all I could produce, week after week, were these poems I called "pandemicals," all in iambic pentameter, all in the same form of sixteen lines and four stanzas each, with fifteen of the poems in rhyme. I do use iambic pentameter a lot in my work, but the persistence of one form and the need to rhyme is unusual for me, as is producing so many poems in such a short space of time. In other words, I felt in the grip of something I had no control over, and in the end, I just gave in to it.

When I look at my pandemicals now, I'm reminded of how stressful 2020 was. Aside from reflections on daily life and on the virus itself, almost all the poems are threaded through with the nightmare of what turned out to be the final year of Donald Trump's presidency. Here, in California, we also had terrible fires—and worse ones in 2021—belatedly seen as highly visible evidence of climate change. The pandemic, the fires, Trump—it all added to my sense of a looming catastrophe. I see now that I *had* to write about it all, not because I wanted to, but because I needed to, with the tight form serving as a container for the chaotic fragments jostling around in my mind.

That's not to say all the pandemicals are fraught. Some are lyrical, some briefly touched by joy. Above all, many display the kind of dark humor that often emerges in a crisis. At first, I wasn't sure why this humorous tone seemed to insist on recurring. I suppose, having grown up in England amid friendly teasing and the kind of sarcasm that can sound insulting to the American ear, a joke or two in the face of trouble comes to me quite naturally. Perhaps that's why Lewis Carroll crept into a couple of poems. Black humor, along with the surreal fantasies and distortions of logic that twist through

Alice's Adventures in Wonderland and *Through the Looking Glass* are not only deeply embedded in my subconscious, but also mirror the freakish quality of our times. "Monty Python's Flying Circus" also comes to mind, its serious silliness not so far removed from contemporary American late night shows. In both, the humor often arises from anger with the status quo. Stephen Colbert's "A Late Show," with its mix of satire and compassion, kept me sane throughout the 2020 lockdown and the non-stop lies and manipulations of the Trump regime.

It might well be these comedic influences that prompted "pandemical" to pop into my head. With the addition of "-ical" the word sounds a bit like "comical," or even like an affectionate diminutive. That's not to lessen the threat of the pandemic. At its best, the companionable comfort of comedy can help us take in the intolerable more easily, while satire's edgy call for truth makes the dark side of life almost impossible to ignore. Ultimately, one can never know exactly why one writes what one does. Humor is not my usual *modus operandi* but in these poems it emerged as instinctively as the sixteen-line form, and seemed as necessary.

Right now, as I write this, the intolerable continues. Covid-19 is no longer simply "the virus." It has spawned a whole range of more deadly variants, with Delta killing unvaccinated people left and right—*and* causing so-called "breakthrough" infections among the vaccinated. Meanwhile, politics everywhere seem to grow more and more toxic. What can we do? I think of William Shakespeare, another wise Englishman for whom (almost five centuries ago!) comedy and tragedy were always intertwined. And I remember the moment in *A Midsummer Night's Dream* when Theseus, Duke of Athens, chuckles over the absurd description of the little play about Pyramus and Thisbe, put on by some hardworking Athenian laborers, that he and his court are about to watch. He is intrigued:

> "Merry" and "tragical?" "Tedious" and "brief?"
> That is hot ice and wondrous strange snow!
> How shall we find the concord of this discord? (5. 1. 62)

How, indeed. As we ponder the "discord" of our own times and despair of finding "concord" between so many disputatious constituents, both viral and human, I have no comforting words to offer, except that *A Midsummer Night's Dream* ends with the *possibility* of harmony and happiness, and that "possible" is a good word to carry around with you.

—Charlotte Innes Los Angeles
September 2021

About the Author

Charlotte Innes is the author of *Descanso Drive,* a book of poems (Kelsay Books, 2017) and two poetry chapbooks, *Licking the Serpent* and *Reading Ruskin in Los Angeles,* both published by Finishing Line Press. Her poems have appeared in many publications. In the U.S., that includes *The Hudson Review, The Raintown Review, Rattle, The Sewanee Review, Tampa Review* and *Valparaiso Poetry Review.* In the U.K., you can find her poems in *Agenda* (online), *Antiphon, The High Window* and other magazines. She has also been published in *Pratik,* Nepal, and a number of anthologies, including *Wide Awake: Poets of Los Angeles and Beyond* (Beyond Baroque Books, 2015) and *The Best American Spiritual Writing for 2006 (Houghton Mifflin, 2006).* A former teacher, newspaper journalist and freelance writer on books and the arts for many publications, including *The Nation* and the *Los Angeles Times,* she currently tutors students in English and creative writing. Originally from England, Charlotte Innes now lives in Los Angeles.

Made in the USA
Columbia, SC
27 December 2021

52615387R00026